DRUM SOLOS AND FILL-INS
FOR THE PROGRESSIVE DRUMMER

BY

TED REED

Published By

TED REED

CLEARWATER, FL 34617

P.O Box 327

Foreword

It has been the ambition -- at one time or another -- of virtually every drummer to be able to play a good sounding extended drum solo, both technically and musically. Many drummers acquire a great deal of technic, and are able to play an extended solo. Technically, it is very good, but it lacks continuity and therefore, does not sound musical. Having the ability to do both, seems to be a gift of a chosen few. Every drummer (with a little help) should be able to play good short solos, particularly "four bar solos". It is hoped, then, that this book will serve just that purpose.

Having mastered these solos, the writer suggests you form some of your own. Keep them simple and tasteful --- never overplay.

You will note all these solos will retain good sound, even though played a little faster or slower than the tempo indicated.

The following abbreviations are used for all drum solos and fill-ins.

Cym. X -------- Strike large ride cymbal with tip of stick.
S.T. Small tom-tom.
S.D. Snare drum.
L.T. Large tom-tom.
B.D. Bass drum.

R on L

X Cross right on left. (stick shot)

All accented notes for the snare drum are rim shots.

After you have mastered each solo, precede and follow it with four bars of basic rhythm, as follows;

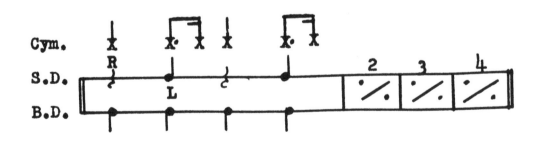

FILL-INS

We are all mindful of the importance of fill-ins in to-day's modern drumming. Therefore, the last 13 pages of this book dwell on fill-ins.

The drummer, as you know, must use good judgment in his/her choice or use of fill-ins. Use them only where they "fit". To repeat - never overplay.

Solo No. 1

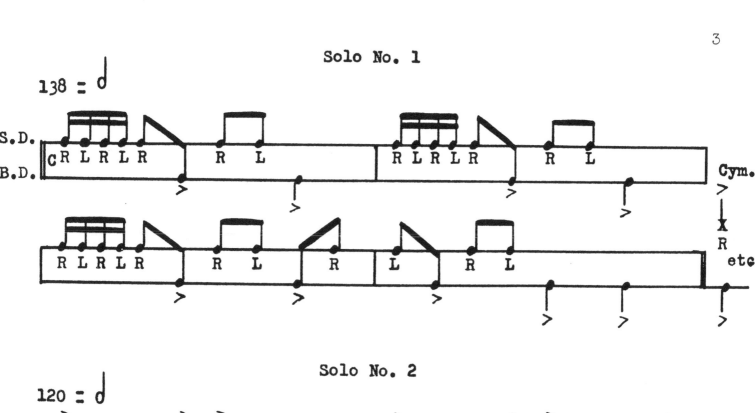

Solo No. 2

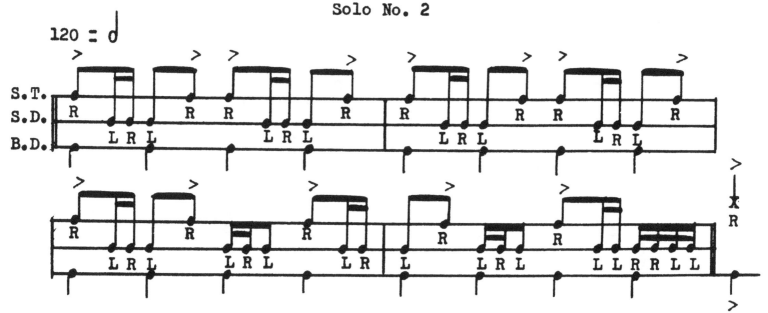

Solo No. 3

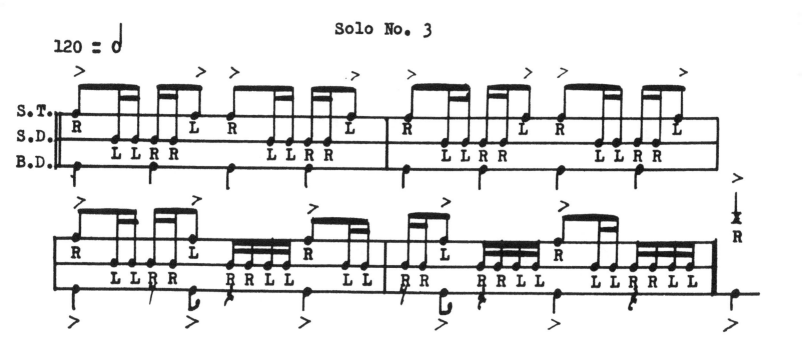

4

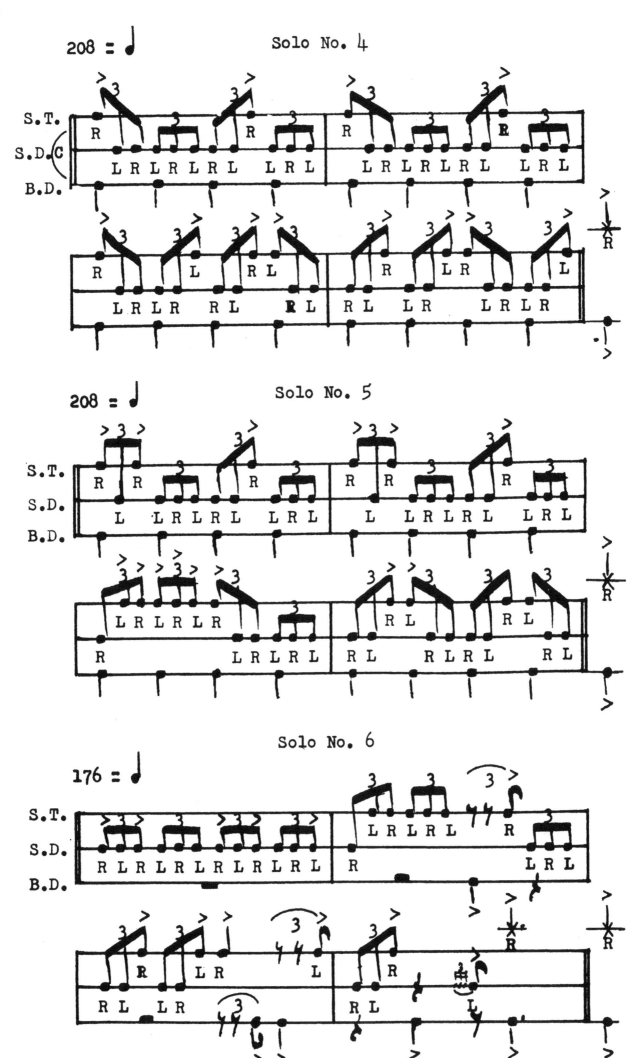

Solo No. 7

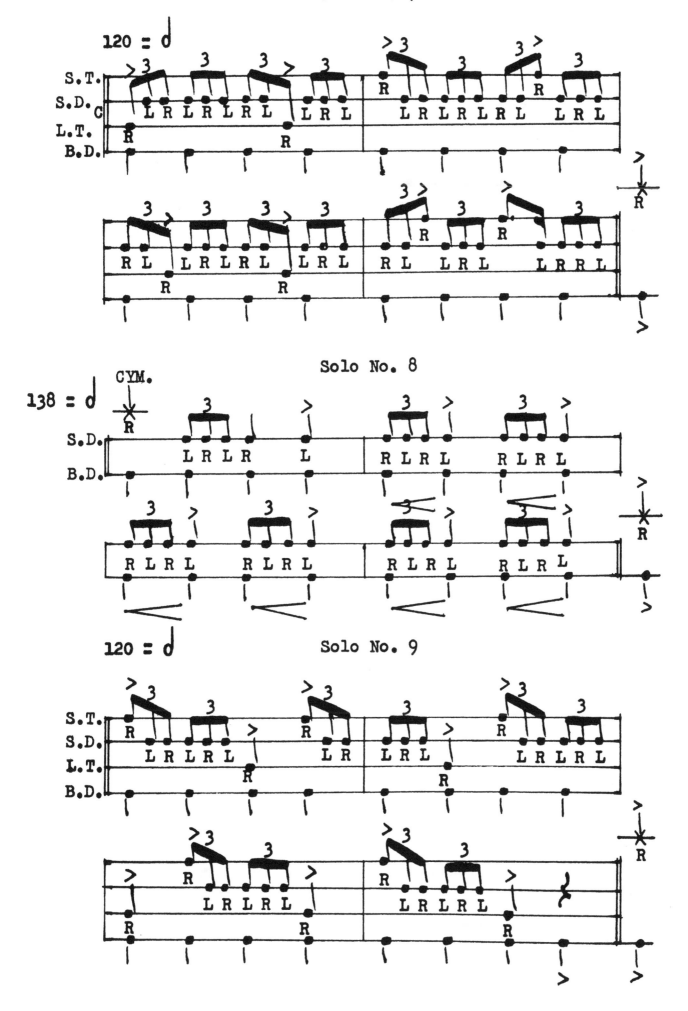

Solo No. 8

Solo No. 9

6

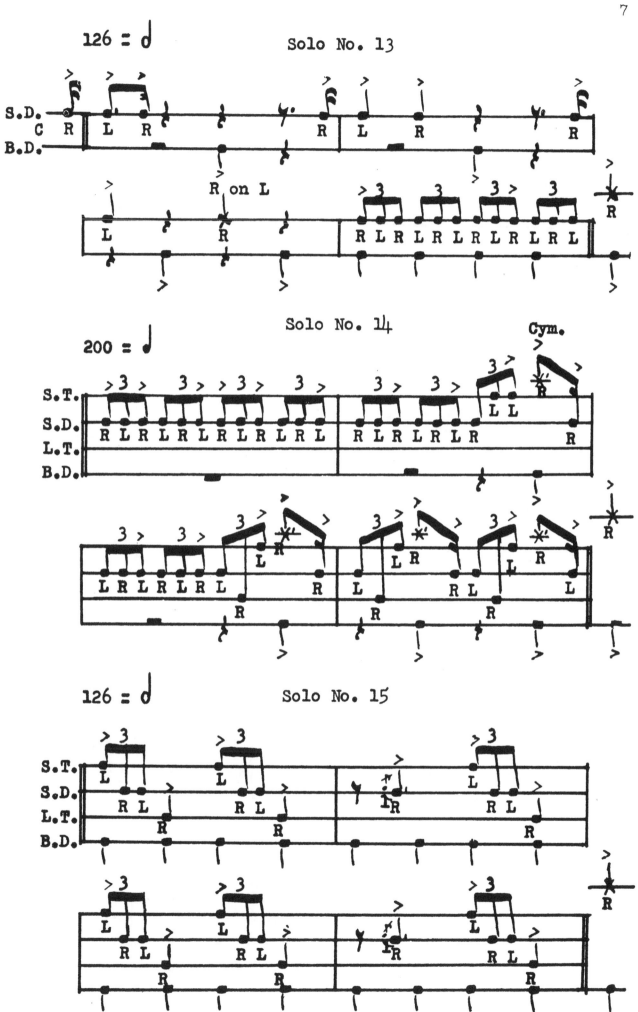

8

Solo No. 16

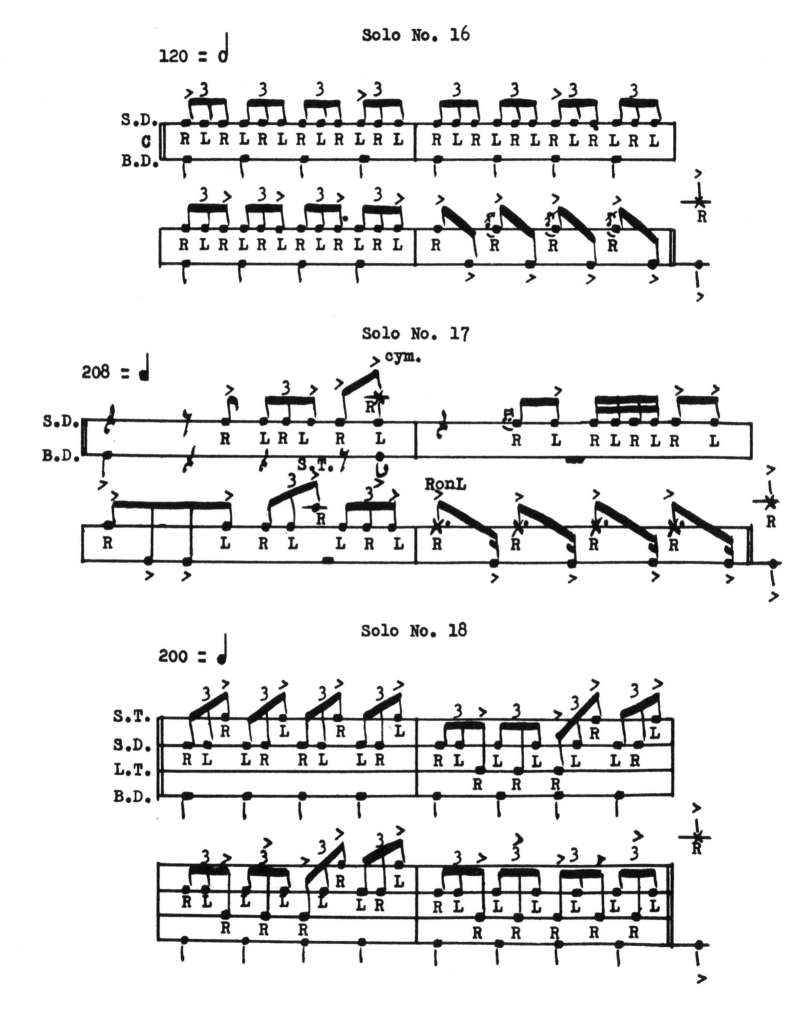

Solo No. 17

Solo No. 18

Solo No. 19

Solo No. 20

Solo No. 21

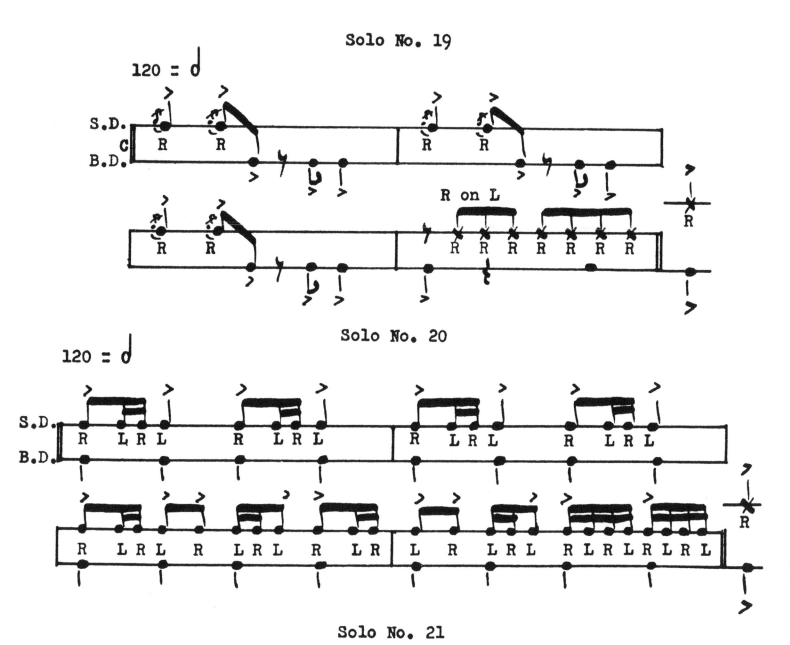

10

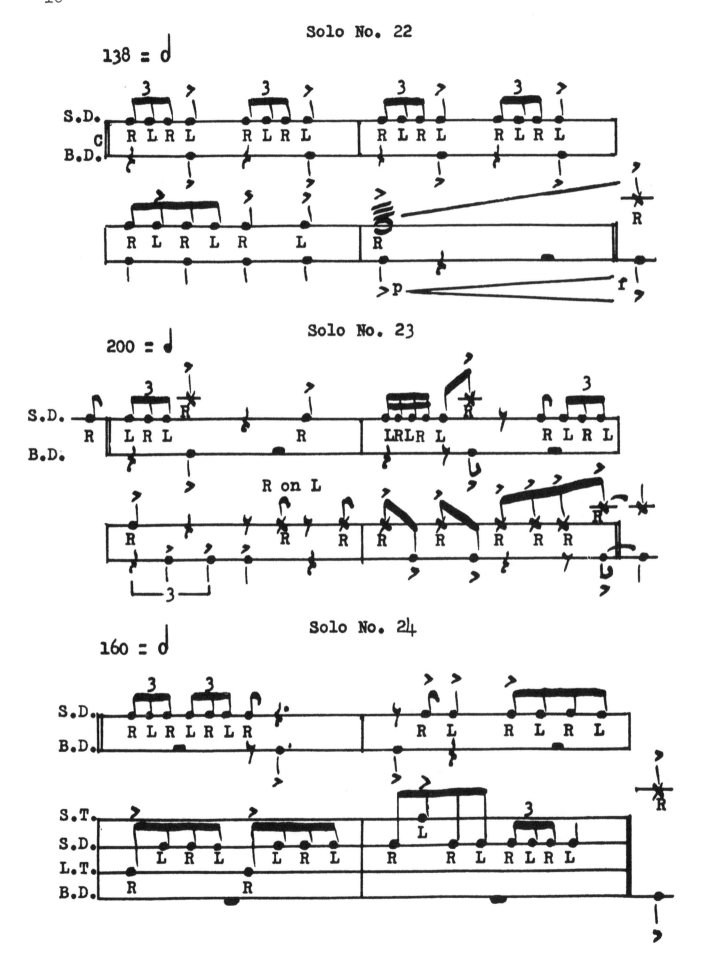

Solo No. 23

Solo No. 24

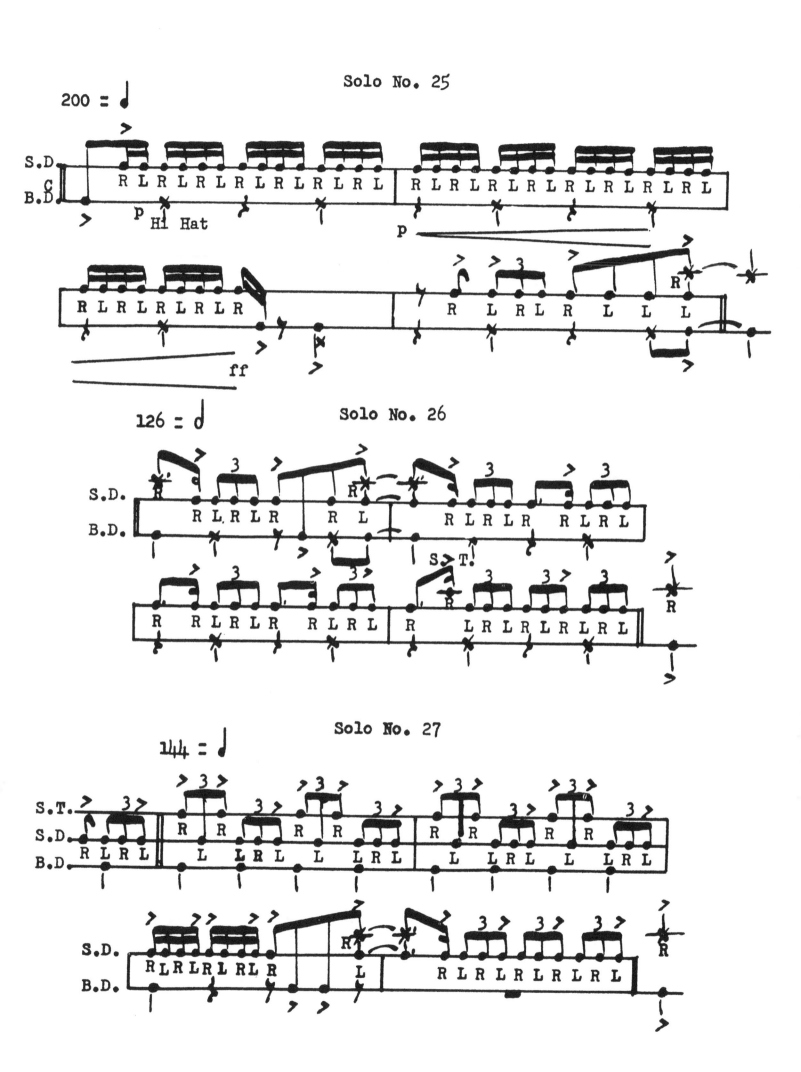

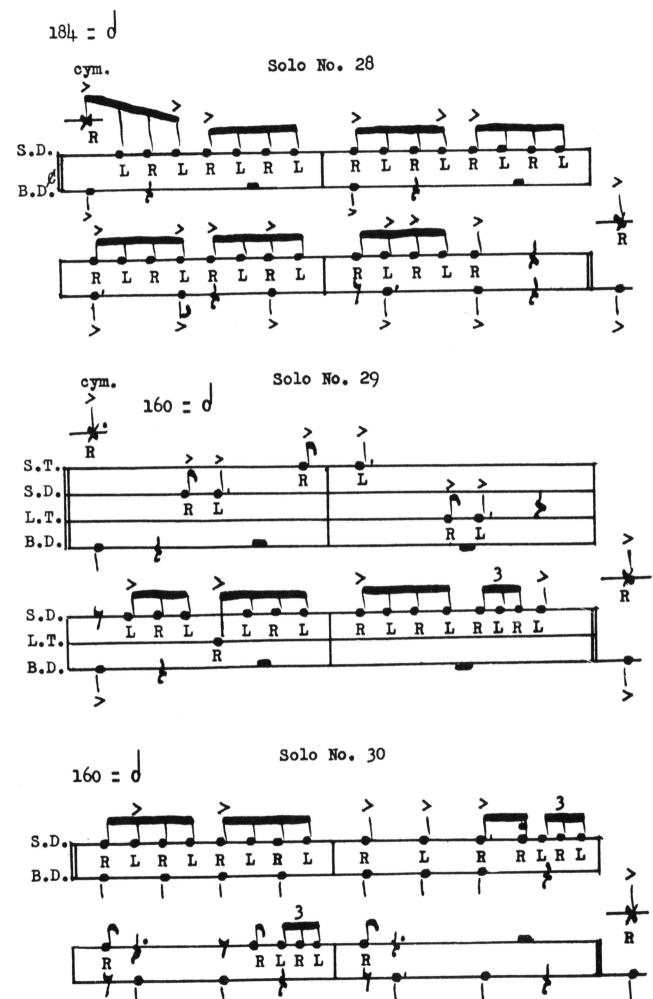

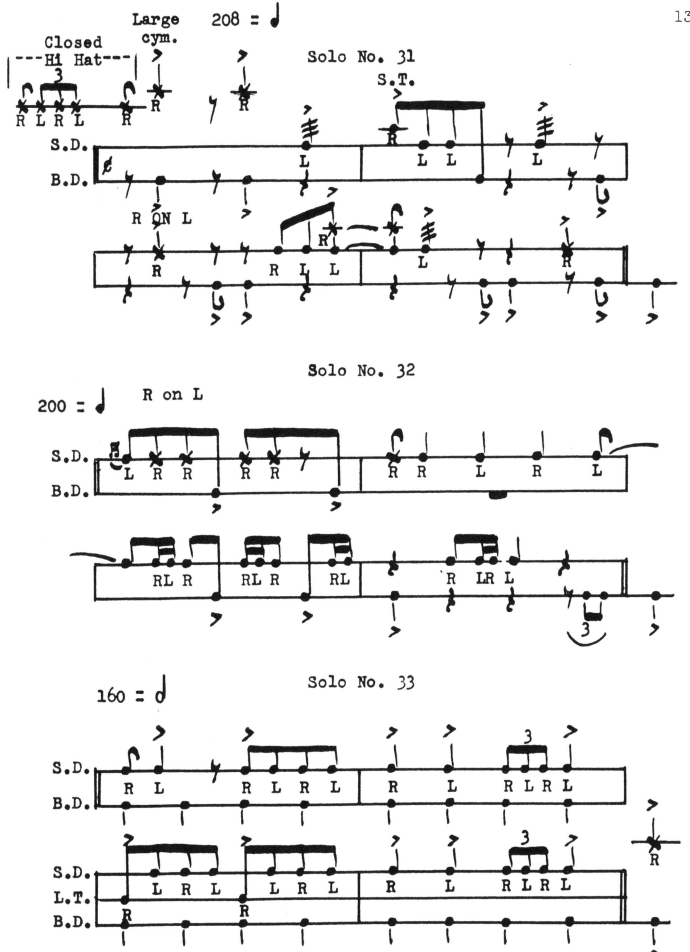

Solo No. 31

Solo No. 32

Solo No. 33

Solo No. 34

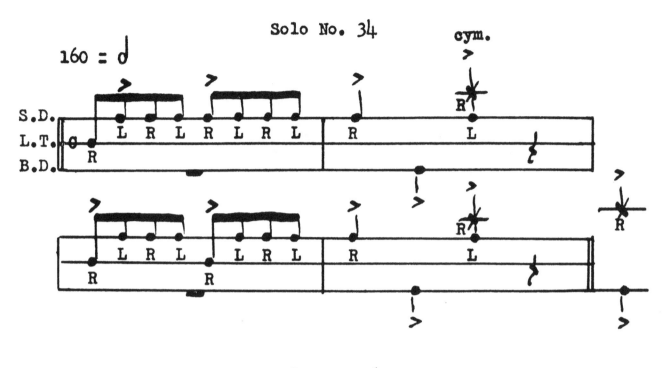

Solo No. 35

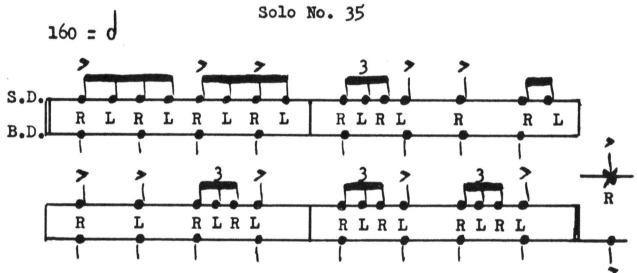

Solo No. 36

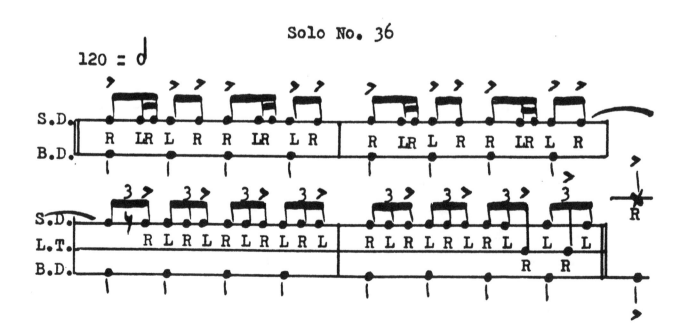

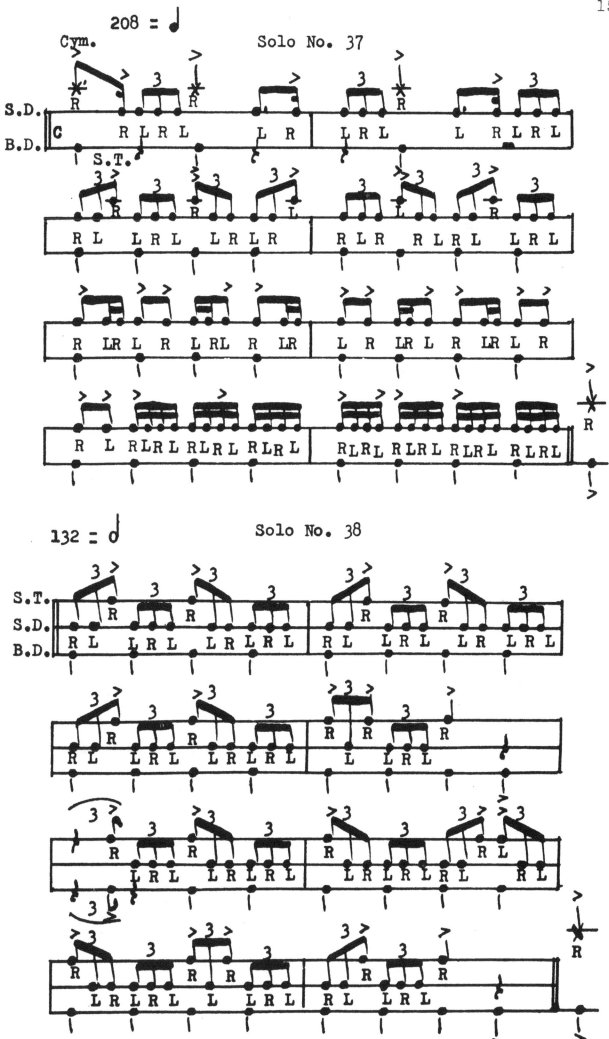

200 = ♩   Solo No. 39

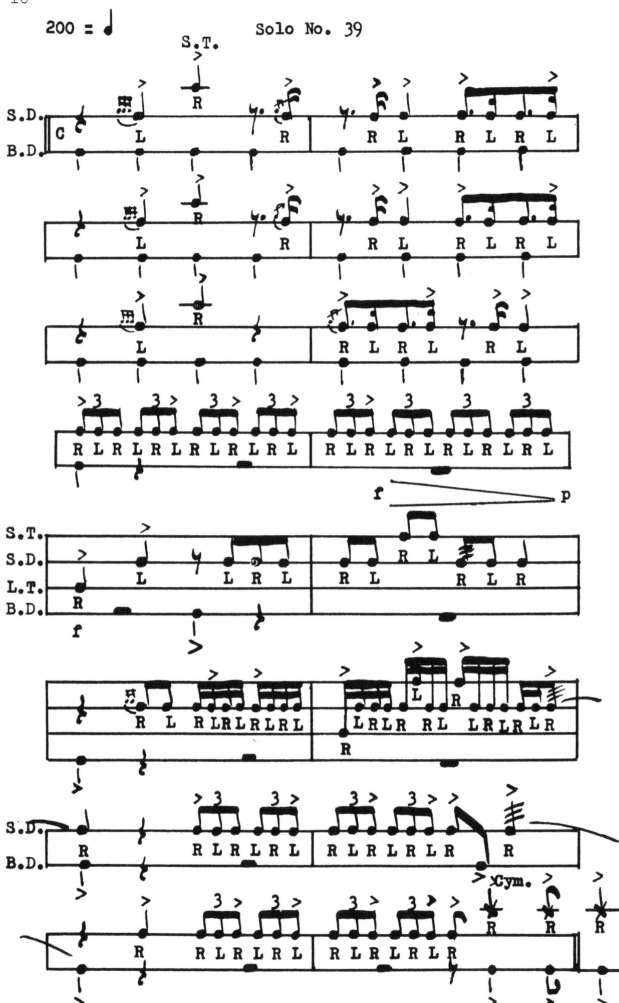

Solo No. 40

18

Solo No. 41

Solo No. 42

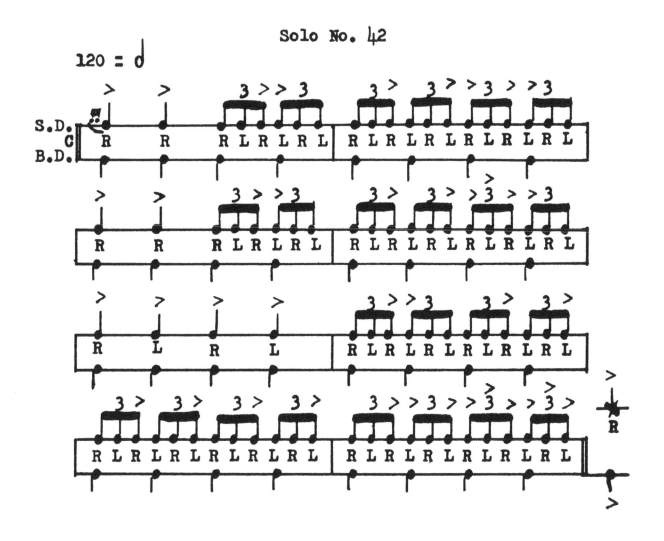

Solo No. 43

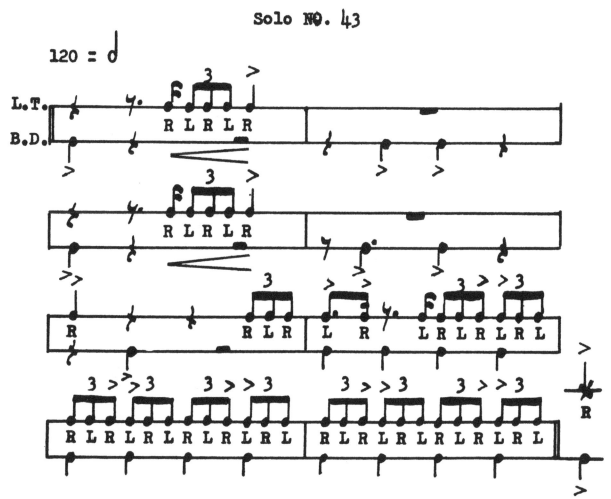

FILL-INS

No. 1
Basic rhythm

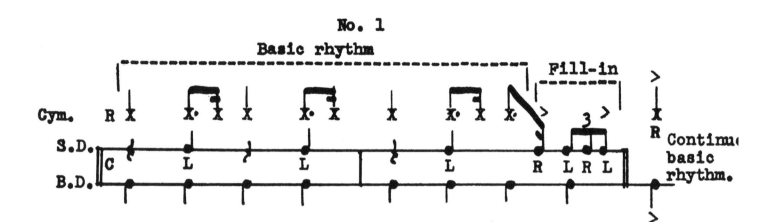

No. 2

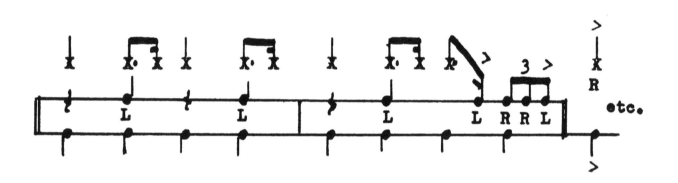

No. 3

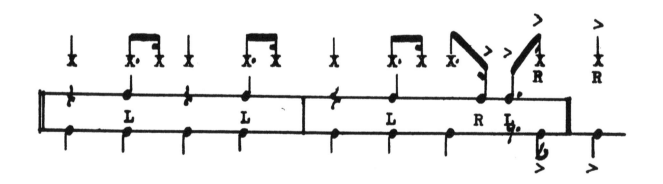

No. 4

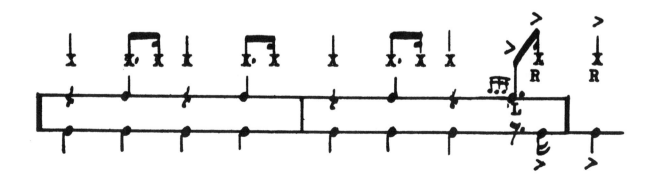

No. 5

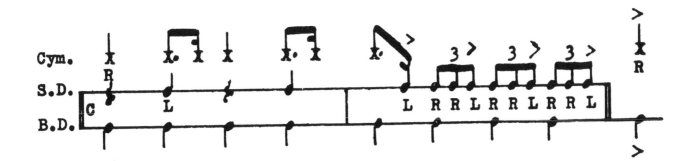

No. 6

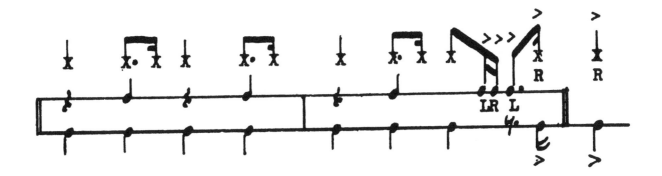

No. 7

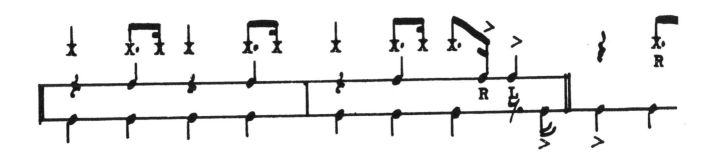

No. 8

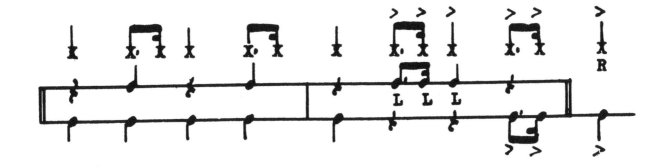

No. 9

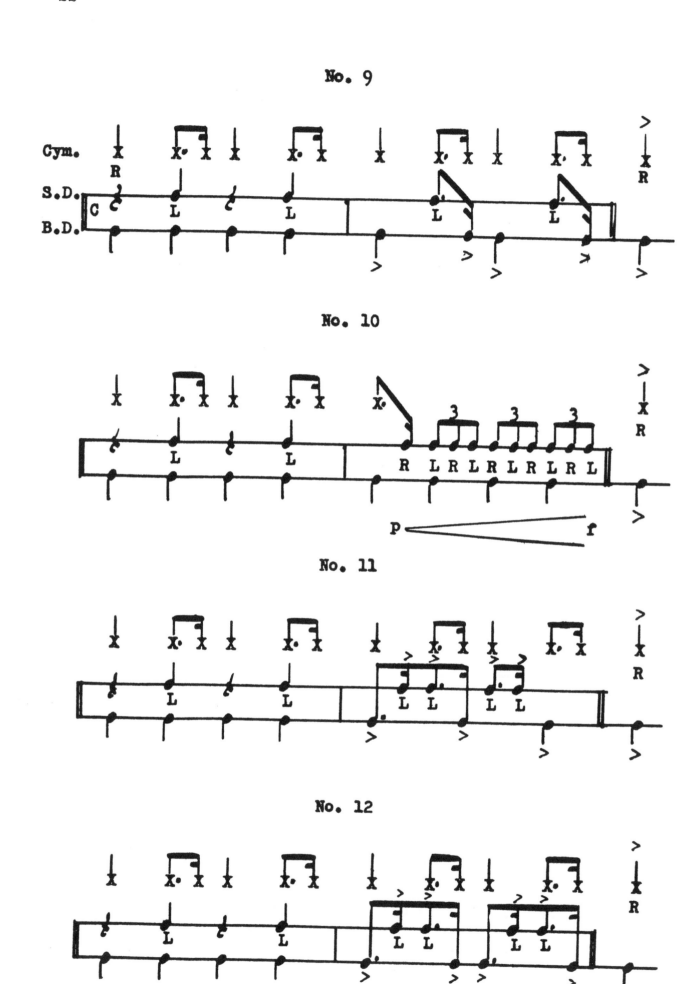

No. 10

No. 11

No. 12

No. 13

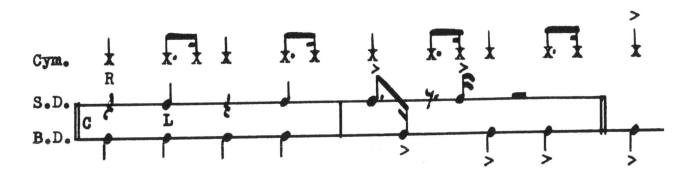

No. 14

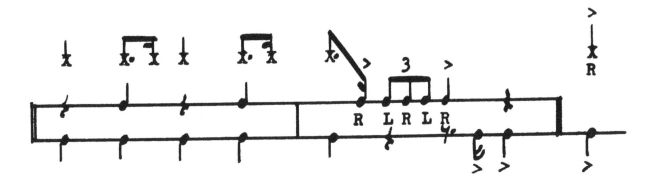

No. 15

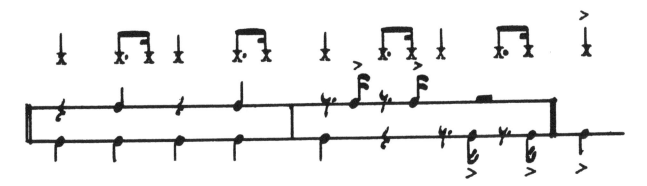

No. 16

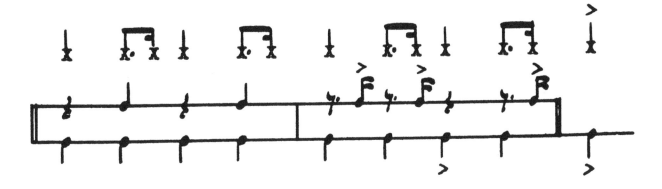

No. 17

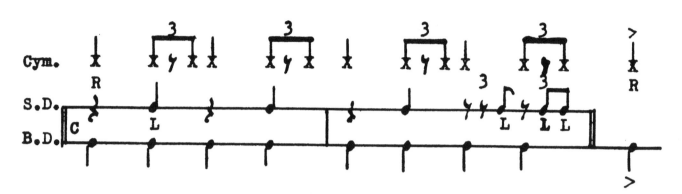

No. 18

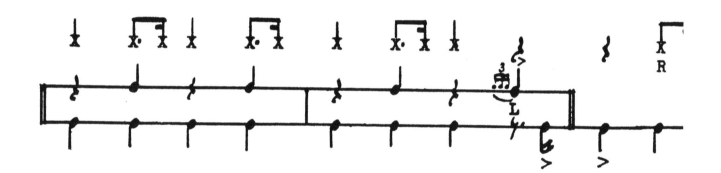

No. 19

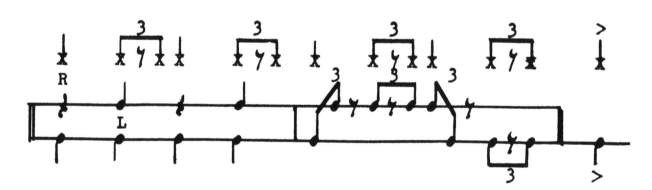

No. 20

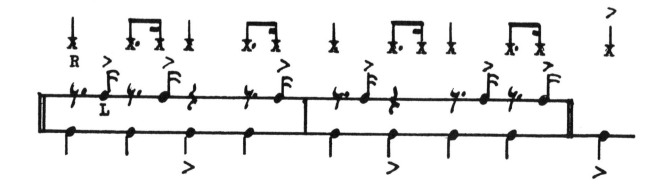

No. 21

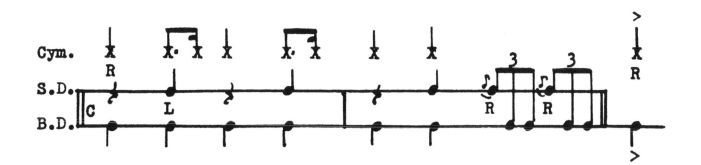

No. 22

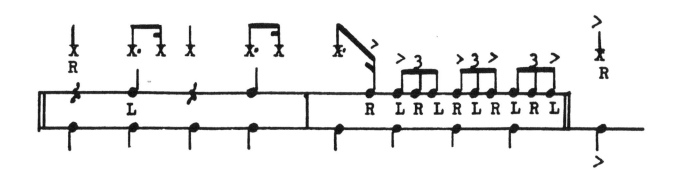

No. 23

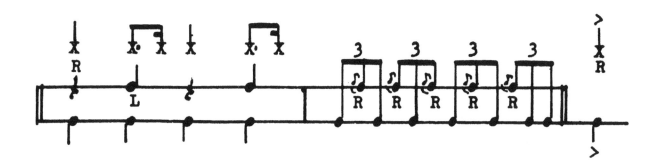

No. 24

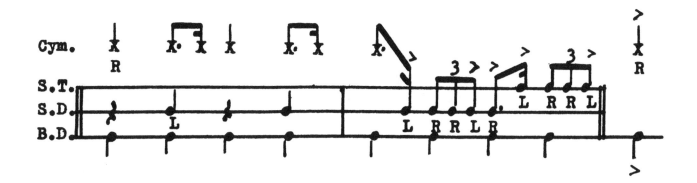

No. 25

No. 26

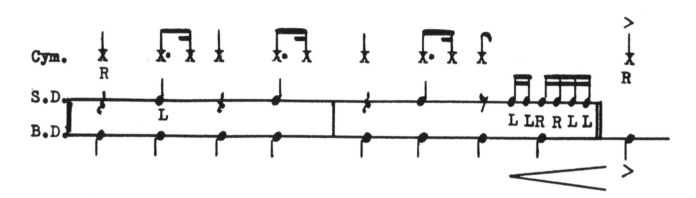

No. 27

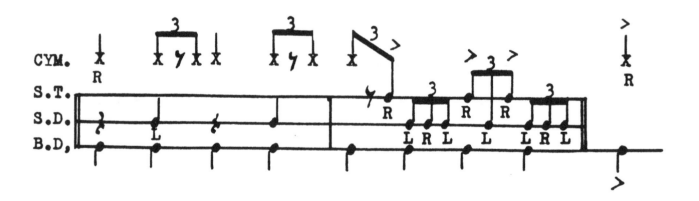

No. 28

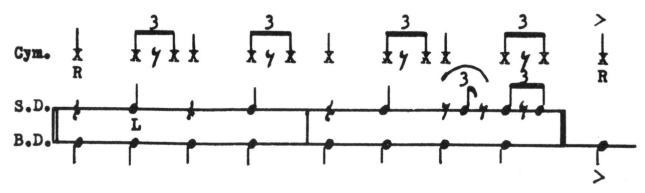

No. 29

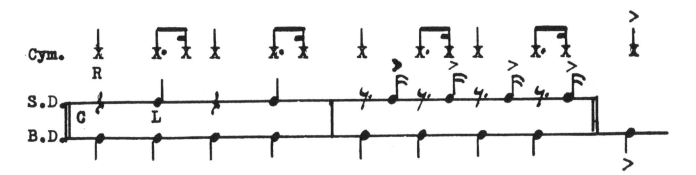

No. 30

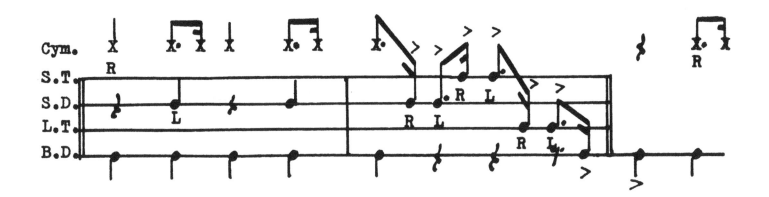

No. 31

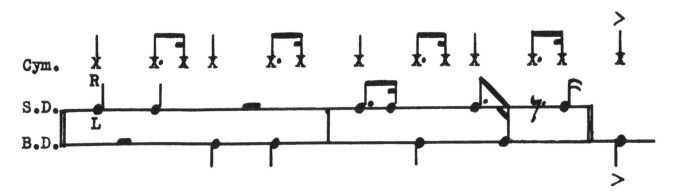

No. 32

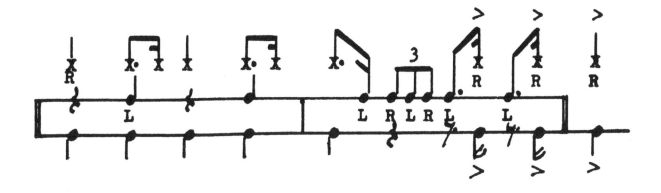

No. 33

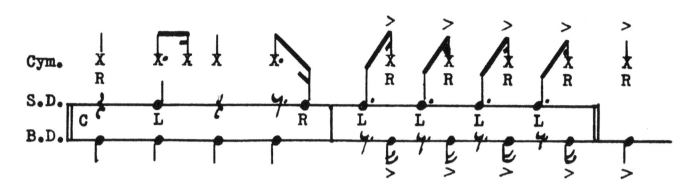

No. 34

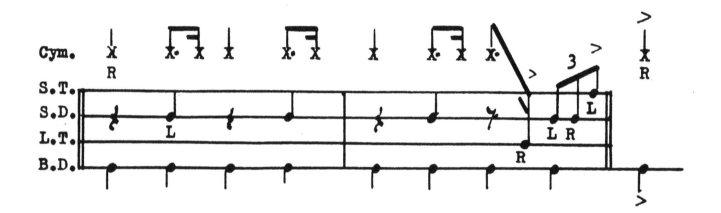

No. 35

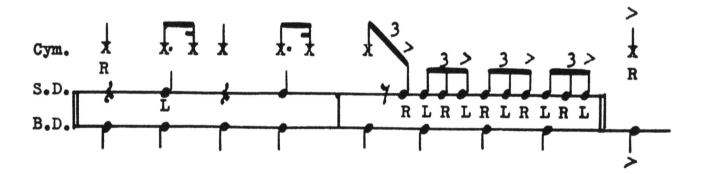

No. 36

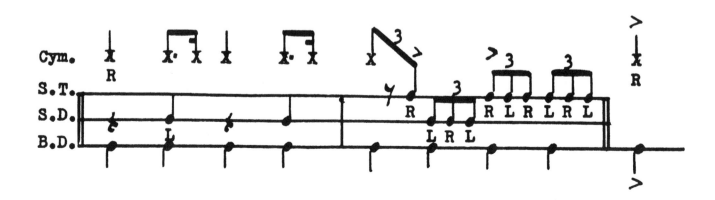

No. 37

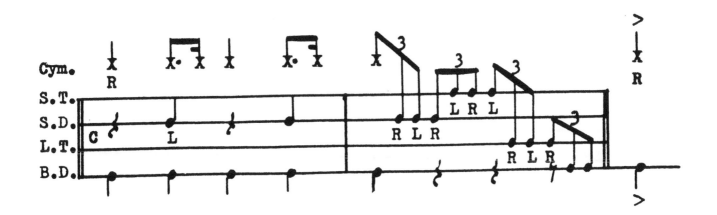

No. 38

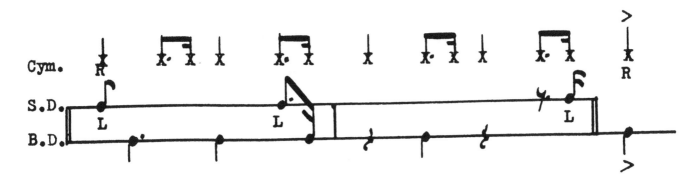

No. 39

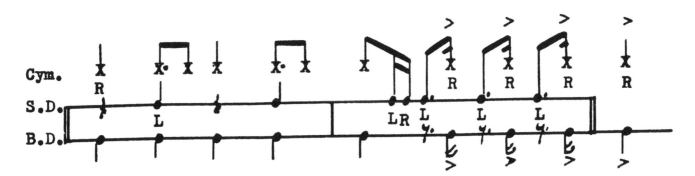

No. 40

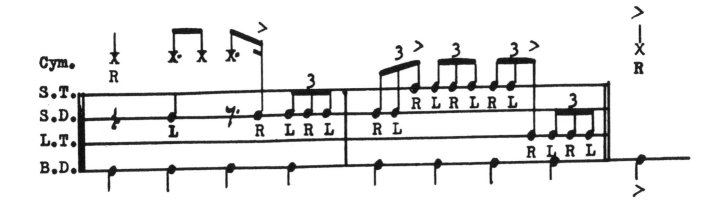

No. 41

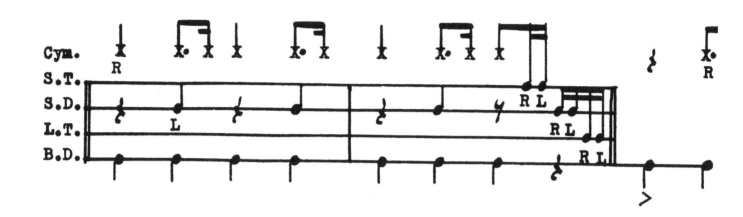

No. 42

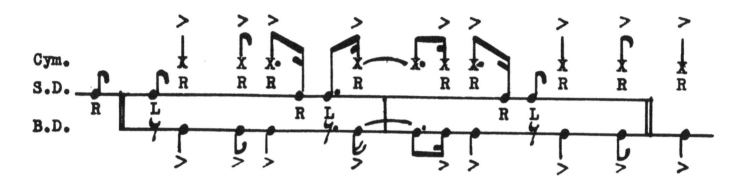

No. 43

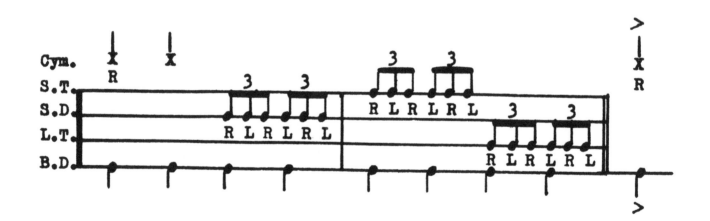

No. 44

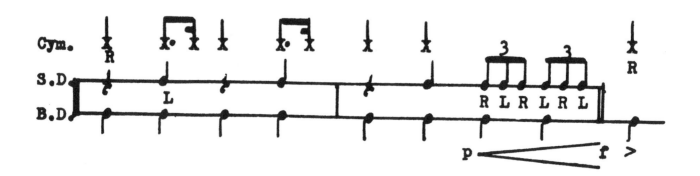

No. 45

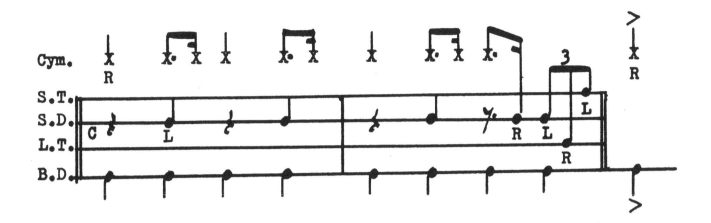

No. 46

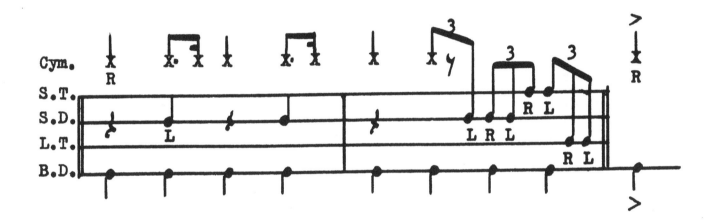

No. 47

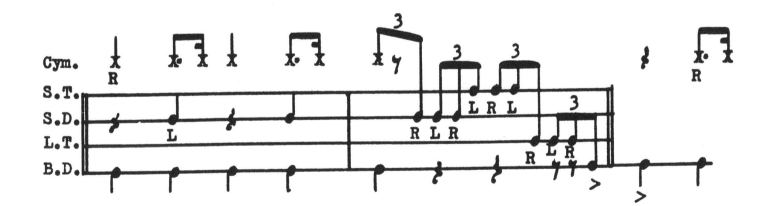

No. 48

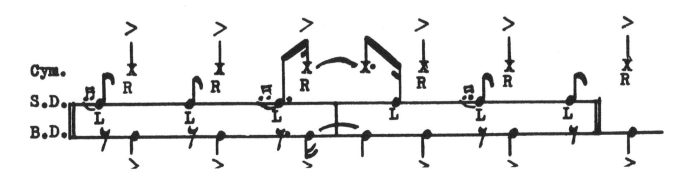

No. 49

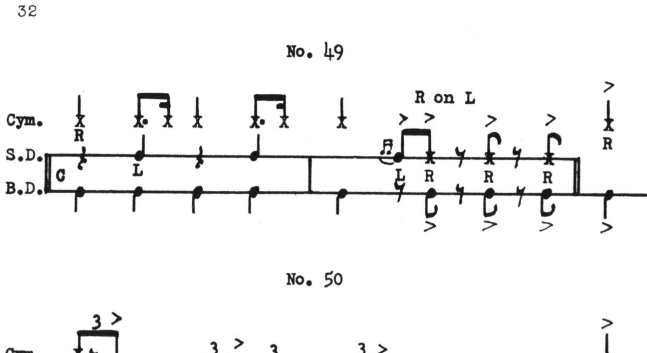

No. 50

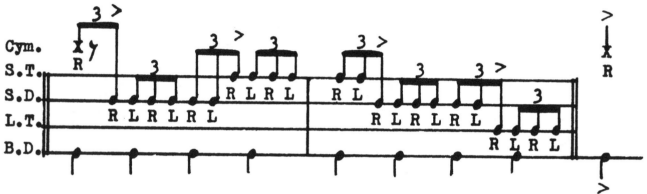

No. 51

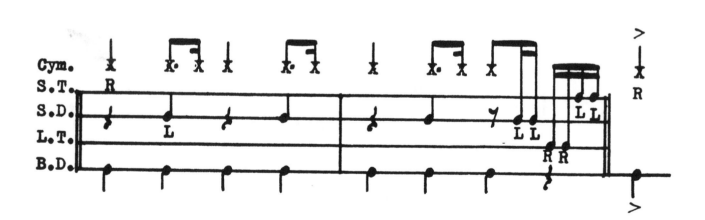

No. 52

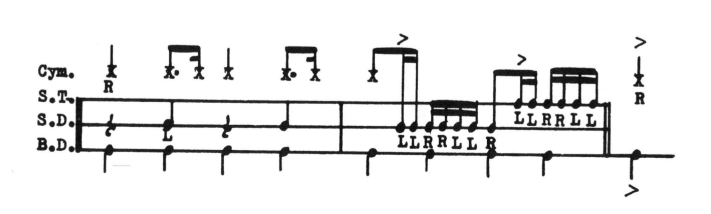